REVOLUTIONARY PATIENCE

REVOLUTIONARY PATIENCE

Dorothee Sölle

Translated by Rita and Robert Kimber

ORBIS BOOKS

Maryknoll, New York 10545

Third Printing, May 1984

Originally published as *meditationen & gebrauchstexte* (1969) and *die revolutionäre geduld* (1974)

Copyright © 1969 and 1974 by Wolfgang Fietkau Verlag, Berlin

English translation copyright © 1977 by Orbis Books

Orbis Books, Maryknoll, NY 10545

Library of Congress Cataloging in Publication Data

Sölle, Dorothee.
    Revolutionary Patience.

    Originally published as Meditationen & Gebrauchstexte
(1969) and Die revolutionäre Geduld (1974)
    I. Title.
PT2681.033A25   831'.9'14   77-24313
ISBN 0-88344-439-9

Contents

vi

REVOLUTIONARY PATIENCE

When he comes again

1   I can't promise you for sure
I have nothing definite to go on
sectarian illusions fill me with sadness
and I recall the faith of my fathers with scorn

Who will come again I would ask
cock robin or humpty dumpty
the singsong of children waking early
the buckets in the abortionist's office

No smile has ever returned
no angel come twice
no peace will come again

If he comes again
I can't promise you for sure
but I promise him to you
I with nothing to go on
you without expectation
he without proof
on his return

2   "Shall there be evil in the city
and the lord hath not done it"
will even one aborted child stir again
will even one soldier frozen to death sing again
will even one lifer be pardoned
will even one doll be made whole again

Will even one smile cross an empty face
will tears dry
will the stench ever fade
between cracow and katowice
will a stone once fallen ever rise again
or a bolt of lightning or a polluted rain
can what is sold belong to no one
can what is used up be unused

AGAIN a word from the new language
we'll need it
when our golden trumpets
bring the walls down

All walls

3   When he comes again
you'll shed your old self

Take the facts of your daily life
the thin walls of your apartment
forbade you to listen
the confines of your desk
forbade you to see clear
the crowded streetcars
forbade you to sing

A foreman was needed
you'll fill that role
until he comes

4 Only this AGAIN
keeps him alive
childhood's forgotten yearnings
the plight of the maimed
call him home to us
in this wasted land

He leaves the bright heavens
comes
again
condemned
to hang between heaven and earth

And there he remains
he absolves the guards
lets the tortured forget
makes hatred subside
teaches the weary to breathe
the trembling to sleep
the dreamers to act
the doers to dream

When he came

1   He needs you
    that's all there is to it
    without you he's left hanging
    goes up in dachau's smoke
    is sugar and spice in the baker's hands
    gets revalued in the next stock market crash
    he's consumed and blown away
    used up
    without you

    Help him
    that's what faith is
    he can't bring it about
    his kingdom
    couldn't then couldn't later can't now
    not at any rate without you
    and that is his irresistible appeal

2   They tell me
he has no father
he heals without prescriptions
but nobody says for how long

A hospital for lepers
one with a lab
is worth more
than his well-intentioned efforts
and the new strain of wheat
that grows undeterred in sand
doesn't that make a nicer story
than the two fish
that fed five thousand
what's so special about him
what singles him out
and who

3   He gave answers to questions they didn't ask
sometimes they didn't dare
open their mouths anymore
not because they hadn't understood
he was taking from them
everything sacred and safe
he offered no guarantees

Fire was not sacred to him or neon
not singing or silence
not fornication or chastity
in his speech foxes breaddough
and much mended nets became sacred
the down and out were his proof
and actually he had as much assurance
of victory as we in these parts do

None

4   Go ahead and compare him with other great figures
socrates
rosa luxemburg
gandhi
he'll stand the test
it would be better of course
if you compared him
with yourself

5   It's supposed to show greatness
     that he didn't say anything
     when they took him prisoner
     when they shoved him into the room
     when they shone a light in his face
     when they questioned him
     when they testified against him
     when they lied about him
     when they lied about his father
     when they lied about his mother
     when they lied about his brothers
     when they lied about his sisters
     when they lied about his intentions
     that he didn't say anything
     is supposed to show greatness
     I don't know

     When they lie about him
     I want to scream

6   He sweats blood
that's why he says
don't cry

He is abandoned
that's why he says
don't give up

He is sold
that's why he says
don't keep accounts

He is condemned
for heaven his cause
that's why he says
look to earth

He is afraid
of yesterday of today of me of them
that's why he says
don't be afraid

7   I like as you have noticed
     to bring things down to earth
     miraculous loaves obedient waves
     even the deathbeds of children
     lying asleep
     they occur
     in the stories of ancient peoples

     Go ahead cut him down to size take away
     the loaves the sea the halt and the lame
     you'll get them back
     when you begin
     to see with his eyes
     every day
     cripples start out
     for his kingdom
     the blind
     begin to see

     All his miracles
     become the most natural thing in the world
     if we make them come about

8   You'll find it hard to believe
what he said
he said and I wouldn't dream
of identifying with this view
wouldn't even consider it worthy of debate
he said those who suffered
were well off
he congratulated the hungry
he put the nihilists in charge
he promised the earth to those
called undesirable in all camps
those behind barbed wire he committed
to hunger poverty despair
to be cheated and sold

9   Dwelling up to their eyes in mud
     paralyzed by fear
     limbs deadened by pain
     blinded by memories

     He called them blessed

     Knocked crutches away from cripples
     that he might call them blessed too

10   I don't as they put it believe in god
but to him I cannot say no hard as I try
take a look at him in the garden
when his friends ran out on him
his face wet with fear
and with the spit of his enemies
him I have to believe

Him I can't bear to abandon
to the great disregard for life
to the monotonous passing of millions of years
to the moronic rhythm of work leisure and work
to the boredom we fail to dispel
in cars in beds in stores

That's how it is they say what do you want
uncertain and not uncritically
I subscribe to the other hypothesis
which is his story
that's not how it is he said for god is
and he staked his life on this claim

Thinking about it I find
one can't let him pay alone
for his hypothesis
so I believe him about
god

The way one believes another's laughter
his tears
or marriage or no for an answer
that's how you'll learn
to believe him about life
promised to all

Remember gotama

Remember gotama scion of a wealthy family
who grew up so sheltered not to say muffled
that in his eighteenth year during a walk in the park
he took fright for his life
never to recover
he saw there four figures
you too have been protected from
sickness
hunger
old age
and death
one of these alone was enough
to crumble the walls of the garden
to lay waste the park
and to turn the golden stones of gotama's dress
black for all time

Since the figures were four and not to be overlooked
and since a handful of rice was no help
the old man was toothless
nor words of consolation
the hungry man died
nor a bag full of gold
the sick man could not walk
nor forgetting
one was the forgetmenot death

he went forth from his beautiful house
leaving clothes behind and money and honors and a wife
who was young and had just given birth to a child
gotama went away
because he had seen the four

He of whom I want to tell you now
also met the four when he walked in his country
in the caves of nazareth he saw sickness
it announced itself with a rattle
in the desert he met hunger
and he saw old people squatting in vain before jericho
and he met death on the banks of the jordan
when he was baptized by one who was soon beheaded

All of these he encountered
but he did not turn away to the mountains of wisdom
instead he asked all four to supper
they sat at his table
old age hunger sickness and death
they followed him on the dusty roads
where there is no shade for hours
and they stayed with him at night
for I assume he didn't sleep well
most of the time

Blessed saint égalité

BLESSED SAINT EGALITE PRAY FOR US
now and in the hour of our death

FOR ALL a bleeding moon soon blotted out
      ghastly smoke from cooling towers
      a playground next to water-filled craters
      and lilacs acacia and what's-it-called
      the magic red flower
      that unlocks the mountain
FOR ALL the fear of swift-striking cancer
      sticky sweat in the palm of the hand
      hunger for all not just for half of humanity
      for all the right to laugh to cry
      dead sons and brothers for all not just for many
      for each a candle here and in a strange country
      for each a fiddler on the roof
      to remind him how different things can be
FOR ALL a beam of wood with nails
      and someone loyal till golgatha
FOR ALL a ringing hallelujah
      chanted by all the dead
      screamed by all the tortured
      stammered by all lovers

O REX NAZARENUS
      you who sound the alarm to the world
      and sing the psalm of the outcast
      and play with the bones of the dead
SEND US THE GREAT DAY FOR ALL
      the wind that sweeps the black streets
      whips up great laughter
      the black trumpeter birds
      fattened by carrion and sun
FOR ALL life and more life
      and learning to die now and
      in the hour of our death
      and loving life now and
      in the hour of our death
FOR ALL one god
      who sends rain and drought
      who damages and inspects
      builds and razes
      here and everywhere

Credo

I believe in god
who did not create an immutable world
a thing incapable of change
who does not govern according to eternal laws
that remain inviolate
or according to a natural order
of rich and poor
of the expert and the ignorant
of rulers and subjects
I believe in god
who willed conflict in life
and wanted us to change the status quo
through our work
through our politics

I believe in jesus christ
who was right when he
like each of us
just another individual who couldn't beat city hall
worked to change the status quo
and was destroyed
looking at him I see
how our intelligence is crippled
our imagination stifled
our efforts wasted
because we do not live as he did

every day I am afraid
that he died in vain
because he is buried in our churches
because we have betrayed his revolution
in our obedience to authority
and our fear of it
I believe in jesus christ
who rises again and again in our lives
so that we will be free
from prejudice and arrogance
from fear and hate
and carry on his revolution
and make way for his kingdom

I believe in the spirit
that jesus brought into the world
in the brotherhood of all nations
I believe it is up to us
what our earth becomes
a vale of tears starvation and tyranny
or a city of god
I believe in a just peace
that can be achieved
in the possibility of a meaningful life
for all people
I believe this world of god's
has a future
amen

Answer to our leftist friends
who ask why we pray

Because we care about the brotherhood
of all
not just of christians or of some other group
of all
those too who will live after us
in our cities with our water
those who bear our mark
unto the third and fourth generation
of all
the dead who lived before us
and whose dreams we betrayed
the dreams of 1789 and of 1917
because we care about our brothers and sisters
     that's why we sometimes say
     OUR FATHER
because our task is never accomplished
and our longing does not diminish in the course of life
because christ does not slake our thirst
but makes it more acute
     that's why we sometimes say
     WHICH ART IN HEAVEN

because we live in places
where some have a say over others
in factories offices and schools
because we know that tyranny
is the most common offense
to the name of god
      that's why we sometimes say
      HALLOWED BE THY NAME
because we fear the vicious circle
of production consumption and profit
for which they try to groom us
      that's why we sometimes say
      THY WILL BE DONE
because we are not without fears about ourselves
not without doubts about ourselves and our way
not without irony toward our own efforts
      that's why we sometimes say
      THY KINGDOM COME
we speak with god
whenever we think about the new world
we talk about daily bread
      and mean the button missing
        on the prisoner's uniform
      and low tariffs on imports from poor countries
we confess our guilt
      as one of the wealthiest countries in a world
      full of starving people
      as citizens intent on order in a country
      full of desperation

we forgive our debtors
     who rob us of life
     respecting their human dignity
     we never stop offering them better suggestions
because we are germans
blind with nationalistic pride mad for revenge
because we ignore the existence of whole countries
and refuse to accept borders of peace
     that's why we sometimes say
     AND LEAD US NOT INTO TEMPTATION
because we are subservient
and have not learned to contain tyranny
and limit the powerful
and barely know how to take charge of our own fate
because we give ourselves up
to resignation and pain
     that's why we sometimes say
     BUT DELIVER US FROM EVIL
because we need faith for the kingdom
we are and we build
and encouragement for our work
so that we don't plan in vain
     that's why we sometimes say
     FOR THINE IS THE KINGDOM
     AND THE POWER
     AND THE GLORY
and count on the fact that god is
FOREVER for us

I've heard

I've heard
that saint thomas
recommended three ways
to combat melancholy
sleeping
bathing
and study of the sufferings of christ

I've noticed
that my friends advise
in such cases
sleeping with someone
drinking
and study of one's own suffering

I imagine
other of my friends
if I could ask them
would recommend
watchfulness
work
and study of a world map
pinpointing illiteracy
and manufacturers of arms

But these friends
whose advice could help
set me right
live far away
behind walls

In this night

In this night
the stars left their habitual places
and kindled wildfire tidings
that spread faster than sound

In this night
the shepherds left their posts
to shout the new slogans
into each other's clogged ears

In this night
the foxes left their warm burrows
and the lion spoke with deliberation
"this is the end
revolution"

In this night
roses fooled the earth
and began to bloom
in the snow

The three kings

I've thought a lot about
why they went
a major disturbance in the sky
a threefold source of light
in an unexpected place
an unfamiliar star among familiar ones
is that reason enough to set out
on sand-drifted roads
carrying stale water in leather bags
month after month
putting aside for now the question of higher powers
that might have influenced them
I have no grasp of things like that
I would call
what drove them from home
where they must have had it good
I would call
this revolutionary virtue of the modern era
curiosity
this I'd guess is what spurred them on
they wanted to see what was up
to straighten out a new confusion
to account for this unexpected brightness
and incorporate it in the existing order

So they built
a more powerful telescope
it didn't help
didn't clear anything up
the new light just glowed
more brightly than ever
so they chartered
well-to-do as they were
a fair-sized caravan
to run down that star
so they bargained bought organized laid in supplies
mapped out with thoroughness and foresight
their route and watering places
planned to travel at night
so they could promptly modify their plan
in accordance with the somewhat erratic
course of the star
so they set out
on their arduous way to explore
this mysterious disturbance
brought into the world
by light

Were they able to explain this star
did they go home
conscious of a higher order
are they still underway
tracing irregularities
in the heavens and on earth
did they accommodate unexpected brightness
to the everyday twilight around them
or is there a chance
that they accommodated themselves
to amazing light
could it be harnessed if so for what
did they see clearer when they got there
more important still
did they who saw it
change
reports are few
evidence scant
but assuming they did change
I would praise the travelers
and rejoice in them and
if this uncommon light is still shining
look at it long and often
for their sake
hoping fervently
for change

The kings made themselves a telescope

The kings made themselves a telescope
a clumsy thing difficult to move
and not much use on an uncharted journey
through the desert at night undertaken
for the sole purpose
of inspecting a stable

The newsmen reported the story
published the palace gossip
and invented the killing of some 2,000
innocent children
for the sole purpose
of playing up the kings

The people of cologne built a box
enameled and bejeweled
embossed reinforced voluted
a magnificent addition to their collection
for the sole purpose
of sanctifying bones

The lord of clouds wind and weather was fond of a child
that screamed and lay there
for the whole world
unprotected from the cold
and for its birthday he gave it
nothing better occurred to him
an ordinary medium-sized star
for the sole purpose
of making more light a little bit more
in bethlehem
not far from duisburg*

*Duisburg is an industrial city comparable to Pittsburgh. —TRANS.

34

Peace

1   Asked to write a poem about peace
I feel shame for those who ask
do they live on a different planet
what are their hopes
and for whom

Gases meant for rice farmers
have been tested
they can be harmless
if the humidity and the wind
are right

So I'd suggest
we talk about the wind

2   Speaking of the wind
    it can be lenient
    rice plants can be merciful
    sometimes
    how friendly the jungle rain is
    it delays attacks
    and the twenty-fourth of december
    lowers the casualty count
    all these things provide cover
    for st sebastian
    for peace

3   He's leaning against a tree
the wood has been sold
the land leased
the water poisoned
the rain kills birds
somebody takes aim at him
he raises his arms against the black wood
it is not finished

Doubts of the teacher

In the phase of despondency
class wars subside
the fears of men grow
here and there peace is negotiated
nobody asks the people
what kind of peace they want
the hopes of the victims
stray to the occult

In the phase of despondency
my certainty grows
I feel
more and more resilient
I don't waste my time doubting
these days
that lowly jesus is the truth
and the way

In the days of fear
I sing once more
in the days of discord
my peace grows

But what for
if it can't be shared
if it remains invisible
if we can't partake of it with others
if the victims go away empty-handed
what good are these riches

If one can't teach it
is that peace

Blessed saint francis

Blessed saint francis
pray for us
now and in the time of despondency
your brother the water is poisoned
children no longer know your brother the fire
the birds shun us

They belittle you
popes and czars
and the americans buy up assisi
including you
blessed saint francis
why did you come among us

In the stony outskirts of the city
I saw you scurrying about
a dog pawing through garbage
even children
choose a plastic car
over you

Blessed saint francis
what have you changed
whom have you helped

Blessed saint francis
pray for us
now and when the rivers run dry
now and when our breath fails us

Exercise in concentration

If I'm absolutely still
I can hear the surge of the sea
from my bed
but it isn't enough to be absolutely still
I also have to draw my thoughts away from the land

It isn't enough to draw one's thoughts away from the land
I also have to attune my breathing to the sea
because I hear less when I breathe in

It isn't enough to attune one's breath to the sea
I also have to ban impatience from my hands and feet

It isn't enough to calm hands and feet
I also have to give up images

It isn't enough to give up images
I have to rid myself of striving

It isn't enough to be rid of striving
if I don't relinquish my ego

It isn't enough to relinquish the ego
I'm learning to fall

It isn't enough to fall
but as I fall
and drop away from myself
I no longer
seek the sea
because the sea
has come up from the coast now
has entered my room
surrounds me

If I'm absolutely still

I can't talk about you

I can't talk about you jesus
I sound ridiculous
you're not to be found
in the huge cathedral built in your honor
in the little corner bar
you're considered a crackpot though a loveable one

My clever friends tell me
you won't get anywhere with that stuff
it's passé
you've got to find other means
to the same ends
my simple friends tell me
you've got to be more patient
my enemies if they knew
how discouraged I am
would rub their clerical hands

I can't talk about you jesus
you aren't enough you're used up
you can't cut it you're alone
you're ambiguous you're for sale
every bishop sleeps with you

I am like the voice of a man
who tries all night to shout down the megaphones
tries to be heard over the insipid muzak
piped into the tourist center
who invokes ancient words
in his mother tongue against statistics
who only twists and knots the telephone cord
in response to desperate calls

I can't talk about you jesus
I trust
my simple friends more than the clever ones
because they pay dearer for everything

But their consolation doesn't help me

Bible stories continued

1. Song on the road to emmaus

So long we have been walking
away from the city of our hope
to a village where life is said to be better

> Hadn't we thought
> we could overcome fear
> the fear of the old pieceworker
> that she'll have to take sick leave
> the fear of the turkish girl
> that she'll be deported
> the fear of the haunted neurotic
> that he'll be committed
> forever

So long we have been walking
in the same wrong direction
away from the city of our hope
to the village where there's supposed to be water

Hadn't we thought
we were free and could liberate
all those poor devils
the working man's child held back and punished
in school
the adolescent on his motorbike
sent to the wrong work
for life
the deaf and dumb
in the wrong country
at the wrong time
silenced by working
a lifetime
for bread alone

So long we have been walking
in the same direction
away from the city
where our hope is still buried

Then we met someone
who shared his bread with us
who showed us the new water
here in the city of our hope
I am the water
you are the water
he is the water
she is the water

Then we turned around and went
back to the city of our buried hope
up to jerusalem

He who brought water is with us
he who brought bread is with us
we shall find the water
we shall be the water

I am the water of life
you are the water of life
we are the water of life
we shall find the water
we shall be the water

2. *Exodus*

When israel departed from egypt
when oppression came to an end
when they refused to be exploited any longer
when they got rid of the slave drivers
      security became a thing of the past
      things got tough
      consumer goods were scarce
the people grumble
      would to god we had died in the land of egypt
      when we sat by the fleshpots
      and when we did eat bread to the full
      for you have brought us forth into this wilderness
      to kill this whole assembly with hunger

When israel departed from egypt
when the construction workers laid down their tools
and the brickmakers had had enough
of baking bricks for the pharaoh's tombs
      the good life came to an end
      they started worrying about
      where they would wind up
      and what would become of them

the people grumble
> if only we had some meat
> remember the fish we ate in egypt for free
> the cucumbers melons onions garlic
> now all we ever get
> is manna

When israel chose self-rule
> over rule by foreigners
when they opted for the desert
rather than the comfortable cities
when they gave up the sedentary life for a nomadic one
> they didn't find the land
> of which they had sung
> no sign of milk and honey
> there was only a long march
> and many died on it
the people debate
> we've got to decide what we want comrades
> the supermarkets of egypt
> or the march through the desert
> forty years
> permanent revolution

3. Meditation on luke 1

It is written that mary said
my soul doth magnify the lord
and my spirit hath rejoiced in god my savior
for he hath regarded the low estate of his handmaiden
for behold from henceforth
all generations shall call me blessed

Today we express that differently
my soul sees the land of freedom
my spirit will leave anxiety behind
the empty faces of women will be filled with life
we will become human beings
long awaited by the generations sacrificed before us

It is written that mary said
for he that is mighty hath done to me great things
and holy is his name
and his mercy is on them that fear him
from generation to generation

Today we express that differently
the great change that is taking place in us and through us
will reach all—or it will not take place
charity will come about when the oppressed
can give up their wasted lives
and learn to live themselves

It is written that mary said
he hath shewed strength with his arm
he hath scattered the proud
he hath put down the mighty from their seats
and exalted them of low degree

Today we express that differently
we shall dispossess our owners and we shall laugh
at those who claim to understand feminine nature
the rule of males over females will end
objects will become subjects
they will achieve their own better right

It is written that mary said
he hath filled the hungry with good things
and the rich he hath sent empty away
he hath holpen his servant israel
in remembrance of his mercy

Today we express that differently
women will go to the moon and sit in parliaments
their desire for self-determination will be fulfilled
the craving for power will go unheeded
their fears will be unneccessary
and exploitation will come to an end

The emancipation of women

We don't want
to be like the men
in our society
crippled beings
under pressure to excel
emotionally impoverished
molded into bureaucrats
functionalized into specialists
condemned to make good

We don't want
the sexual rights and
the sexual idiocy of men
genital output
measured in quantity
sex for sale
demanded bought
paid for and exhibited

We don't want
the small families
men have invented
and tyrannized

families that live only for themselves
that make women infantile
children neurotic
all apolitical

We don't want
to be supported prettified sheltered
to feed drill break children
coddle and rejuvenate men

We don't want
to learn what men can do
rule and command
conquer and be waited on
hunt capture subdue

The long march

1   Perhaps we pictured things too simply
way back then when we set out
on the long march through the desert
to find better ways to live with each other

O lord we thought let us become
instruments of your peace
but what followed was
tiresome conflict with authorities
that want order not peace
the daily struggle for small victories
and the terrible sense of being abandoned
then the instruments of peace
became disruptive and tiresome obstacles
to harmonious accord

2   Many have known all along
    that nothing can be done from within the church
    who can live on manna year after year
    if he sees no point in what he's doing

    Many are fed up and wish they were back in egypt
    where tithes flowed like milk and honey
    and the churches were filled and the hymns rang out
    loud and clear because everybody knew them

    How much longer is this march to last
    what does that mean forty years
    is it only our generation that will be squandered
    or the next one too and what for
    can the goal justify a whole lifetime
    of work and conferences
    will we ever get beyond numbness
    nothing but sand and stones no human beings
    who will stick with us in our work
    help us speak clearly and openly

    We receive little help from below
    are seldom understood by our peers
    and those above fall back on the old trick
    of deeming any substantive question
    a breach of discipline
    that's how they assert their authority maintain order
    and keep away from the pulpit
    the crude speech of the common people

The desert through which we wander
restless fearful
impotent confused

O lord make us into instruments of your peace
instruments of conflict not harmony
instruments of truth not obfuscation
instruments of happiness not stupefaction

Let's see if that can't be done

3   We have to talk over with you god
what we'll need for peace
we'll need a lot more friends
if we're going to make more peace
friends from different classes
even if they don't read thomas mann
friends from different churches
even if they do have rosaries
friends of both sexes even gays and lesbians
friends with different interests
even if we don't like them
friends who share a vision
of peace that can be achieved
friends who believe

Keep us from the romantic illusion god
that friendships are made in heaven
and from the conservative illusion
that they grow slowly over the years like trees
teach us to see that friendship is work
and has to be built like everything that is good for us

We need friends who are
not putty in other men's hands
who have a voice and a say
who side with the penalized
who grow more and more fearless
and so spread peace

4 Remember our friends in holland
when they realized that coffee
imported from angola
tasted of blood and of the napalm
that was killing frelimos
they taught a whole country
to stop drinking that coffee
everyone there knows what angola is
the vietnam europeans are making in africa

Remember our friends in isolotto
how they celebrate mass under umbrellas
because the church doors are locked
how they spread the gospel to all
unafraid to disturb the false peace*

Remember martin luther king
and the city of resurrection
how they discovered their own strength in marching
in singing in taking a stand
how they left a land of false peace behind

Remember the priests and nuns in brazilian prisons
how water is poured over their heads
to keep them from dying under torture

---

*Don Mazzi, a Catholic priest in Isolotto-Florence, was forbidden, for political reasons, to celebrate Mass with his congregation. —TRANS.

Remember

There is a swarm of witnesses
we see them hear about them
learn friendship from them
we share their vision

5   Remember our friends nearby too
in wanne-eickel rheinhausen*
or anyplace else you think of
many have tried the new way
celebrating singing eating
let us follow the new way
our cause has a tradition
we needn't always beg and do battle
our cause will outlast the bureaucracies

We need friends
maybe we have them already
many can be won for peace
more than we think more than we see
let us follow the old call
and be fishers of men

*Wanne-Eickel and Rheinhausen are mining and industrial cities in the
Ruhr. —TRANS.

When one of my students
committed suicide

I didn't know
you didn't know
he she it we you they
didn't know

I couldn't have known
I didn't want to know
I couldn't see it coming
I let it happen
I couldn't stop it

I have only two eyes
I have only two hands
I have only one telephone
I can't be everywhere
I can't always be reached

I believe in christ people say
he could have helped her people say
when I you he she it we they
have become christ
there'll be no more need
to say people say

Reasons why we can overcome helplessness

We can hold out longer
we need a better future
there are people with worse wounds among us
victims of capitalism
bread enough for everyone
has been passed out among us before

We can hold out longer
we are building the city of man
the disenfranchised behind walls are our allies
and the disinherited in the cities
the dead of the second world war belong to us
they want something to eat at last and justice
one who is of us has risen
from the dead before

Ernesto cardenal

Ernesto cardenal
questioned on how he came to be
a poet a priest
and a revolutionary
gave as his first reason
love of beauty

This led him he said
to poetry
(and beyond)
it led him
to god
(and beyond)
it led him
to the gospel
(and beyond)
it led him
to socialism
(and beyond)

How weak a love of beauty must be
that is content with house beautiful
how trivial a love of poetry
that stops with the text
how small a love of god
that becomes sated in him
not hungrier
how little we love the gospel
if we keep it to ourselves
how powerless are socialistic yearnings
if they fear
to go beyond what will be

Churchyard in housseras
(alfred döblin's grave)

The pile driver on alexanderplatz
and the blue amazon
here the manure spreader rumbles by
people cook with wood here

Buried in the vosges
neither german nor jew
born to the nation of children
and madmen

A son died here "pour la france"
the father and the mother pour quoi
the world is of iron
there's nothing for it

Ribbons and artificial flowers
peasant women's finest baubles
pathetic courageous graves
in the church stove a fire crackles
outside the wall
children shriek
the blue smoke rises straight
too late for cain

Too late for abel
the writer is silent
fiat voluntas tua
was the ideal
he strove for

I'd like to
ask him about that
later

Alfred Döblin (1878–1957) was a German novelist. The first two lines of this
poem refer to his novels *Berlin Alexanderplatz* and *Amazonas*, a historical
novel about the conquest of South America. Housseras is a small village in
the Vosges Mountains of northeastern France. —TRANS.

Imprisoned

Three times I read "corrective institutions"
which we've wanted to reform for a long time
until I noticed
the phrase was "collective institutions"
I started and saw
us all
sitting in the prison
called language

On reading nadeshda mandelstam

The poet
suspected and shadowed for a long time
has friends

One of them hangs up three times
when the marked man calls

Another sends his wife
to ask how things are
he's out of town himself

A third turns informer
he needs a better apartment

When the car came to pick him up
three close neighbors
happened to be sleeping

Denial betrayal abandonment and sleep
the old story of friendship
remember that christ died
for friends like these

A typical dismal morning

I lay awake from three to four
got up quietly not wanting to wake anyone
went into the next room
and read
fell asleep again
until a nightmare
woke me
I made breakfast for the children
the nightmare still with me
because of it
I lay down again
to get a better grip
on myself

Of my voluntary actions
on this dismal morning
most would have been impossible
if I like most women
went to work

Only the lying awake
alongside a snoring man
would have been possible
and the bad dreams
of an aging woman

Travel notes

1. Hospital in haiphong

Doan is three years old
in his head a fragment
of that handy bomb
that leaves buildings undamaged
never puts a factory out of production
doesn't even harm bridges

Doan is three years old
in that handy bomb
are millions of tiny fragments
just for doan
meant for his feet
designed for liver and lung

Doan is three years old
his mother is gone
the president of the united dead
sent her an invitation
to a high standard of living and a lasting peace
he sent a handy bomb

Doan can't write yet
so I'm writing this letter
to the workers in st paul minnesota
asking if they couldn't make
a toy boat out of plastic
instead of bombs because
doan is only three years old

2. Peace

Peace has to seek cover
it's a doctor in a bomb shelter
searching for shrapnel in an infant's lungs
it's a teacher sitting in a cave
showing girls how to defuse bombs
it's a mother squatting in a bunker
nursing her child between shifts

Peace under the earth
not on it

3. *Amendment to §218*

The mat weaver tran van tho
still trembles when he hears a plane
his wife who was drying rice
when the B-52s came
was pregnant

We who in foreign lands
have long fought for voluntary abortion
take sides with the unborn here
and borrowing the words of our opponents
call this killing murder

§218 is the paragraph in German law forbidding abortion. —Trans.

4. The riches of the poor

A child without shoes
his clothes already outgrown
his bicycle missing nuts and bolts
carries delicately
as we would the host
the symbol of life
his inkpot

5. A comparison

In a metal-working factory
in haiphong not far from hanoi
a machinist played a bamboo flute
a girl at a lathe sang
an unskilled worker picked up his guitar

The girl sang of devotion
a song two thousand years old
the machinist played "the joys of victory"
an old story that will begin tomorrow
tears came to my eyes
"thinking about germany in the night"*
about the lathe operators in düsseldorf
and the unskilled workers at siemens
who will never learn to sing
in this life of ours

*A line from a poem by Heinrich Heine: "Denke ich an Deutschland in der Nacht." —TRANS.

6. Different answers

Everywhere we ask
whether it will come tomorrow
or in the spring
or in the spring after that
peace

Khoat an old music professor
everyone knows his songs about struggle and liberation
sends greetings to the children of germany
he urges them to study hard
and write poems too

Tho a twelve-year-old girl
who loves adventure stories
will "avenge my mother
when I'm grown up"

And viên that melancholy and comic poet
pleads with the mother of god
"dear mary you have been carrying your child
in your arms for 1969 years
do you know that vietnamese mothers
are growing older and unhappier day by day"

But pham van dong president of a free people
breaks out in uproarious laughter
against minute hopes for today or tomorrow
hopes just bombed to smithereens again
he sets a simple truth
impervious to bombs
"on n'arrête pas le soleil"

You can't stop the sun

7. *They've stopped bombing*

They've stopped bombing
and coming in low over their targets
swords have still not been made into sickles
but the B-52s are grounded
we laugh and cry
te deum laudamus our fathers sang
how about making another baby
my husband says to me

I can see the petit lac in hanoi
people picking through the rubble
the moon rises behind the pagoda
the loudspeakers play music
and I see the people
laughing
crying
walking arm in arm

Yes I say to them
good reason
for making babies

8. New arithmetic

The mayor of hanoi
nearly bald his face all wrinkles
claims
he is only twenty-seven
he bases that claim
on the age of the republic
ho chi minh taught the citizens
all to be the same age
as old as the cause they love

According to this arithmetic
the mayor's grandchildren
are already twenty-seven
and later people will live
as old books promise
to be a thousand and more

9. Middle-class music

The pianist maurizio pollini one-time prodigy
got the bronx cheer
his concert before an audience of 2,000 in milan
was broken off
cultured patrons in tuxedos and fur capes
members of the quartet society
raged and shouted him down
       back to your piano
       we've paid to hear you play
no provision was made
the concert manager said
for a political speech
he is entitled to his ideas
but he is obliged to play
as stipulated by contract
       back to your piano
       we've paid to hear you play
I had thought maurizio said
they would at least let me finish reading
before they began to protest
I expected a debate
not this kind of aggression
       back to your piano
       we've paid to hear you play

And I had always thought
people loved beethoven
because his music
grew from struggle and suffering
and sang of human dignity
I had heard hanoi was
the metropolis of human dignity
in the world today
rather too late I understand
that the concert audience in milan
and my mother and my brothers
love and buy and
worst of all
hear
quite another beethoven